What Makes the Wave Break?

Toadhouse, a.k.a. Allan Graham, was born in San Francisco, California, in 1943 and passed away in Santa Fe, New Mexico, in 2019. He was an artist whose work includes sculpture, painting, words, and video.

toadhouse

What Makes the Wave Break?

basic rightings (1997-2004)

THIS IS A SNUGGLY BOOK

Copyright © 2020 by the Estate of Allan Graham
All rights reserved.

Edited and compiled by Brendan Connell.

ISBN: 978-1-64525-020-3

Front and back cover art by Allan Graham.

contents

by way of an introduction / *7*

from a notebook (1987-1988) / *17*
from a notebook (1988-1990) / *25*
not two (circa early 90s) / *31*
like leaves (1993) / *61*
phallacy (1994) / *79*
from a notebook (2000) / *91*
from a notebook (2002) / *97*
from a notebook (2003-2004) / *103*

by way of an introduction

Several months before he passed away, Allan Graham, known to many under the pseudonym of Toadhouse, asked me to help him put together a book. I had previously edited and compiled two other books for him, *Gone Fishing with Samy Rosenstock* (2016) and *Living and Dying in a Mind Field* (2017), and I imagined the project he had in mind would be similar.

I asked him several times after that what his idea for this new book was, and, though he clearly wanted to proceed with it, he avoided telling me what the actual contents would be. To fulfill the project, I have therefore used his notebooks and writings to assemble the present volume, very much in the manner that the other two I helped him with were created.

All the words herein are presented as closely as possible to their originals. Only on a very few occasions have I edited a word or line, doing so in a way I feel fairly confident Allan would approve of. These extremely slight modifications, however, could probably be counted on one hand.

Of the various items in this volume, two are from manuscripts printed and then bound in the Japanese manner, one is from a manuscript printed, but left unbound, and the rest are, as the headings indicate, from handwritten notebooks. One of the manuscripts, that titled "not two," exists in a single copy. The other two exist in multiple copies, the versions of each differing somewhat in content, and so some of these selections might well have an item or two different from copies he distributed, if he distributed any at all.

—Brendan Connell

What Makes
the Wave Break?

A single hand held out in the midst of all being.

—Dōgen

I want to say something to you:
something more than being an artist:
something more than success or failure:
more than life as most of us know it.
I want to say something to you that
transcends doubt and willfulness: fear
and ego—free from meaning, free from
intent, free of consequence.

But how?

—Allan Graham
January, '89

from a notebook

1987-1988

(harmonics) outside cause & effect
the area of contaminations
non-duality, outside time and space?
<u>between</u>

one must turn language to twin mind
the revolution of non-deception

movement = moment
   no outside no inside
     now

I forget
  all
    the
      time

white is relative

I use art
to support
the more serious
work
    living

from a notebook

1988-1990

maintaining a
    position
is
an illusion

<u>you are movement
in
all directions</u>—
centered at
any
    point
constantly made
    up—
constantly
    released
time is action revised—
captured containment
denial through
    holding
fear of
    up or down

I move one grain of sand—
    the beach is changed
as the beach is changed
    the wave changes form
as the wave changes form
    the ocean shifts
as the ocean shifts
    the earth adjusts
as the earth adjusts
    the planets coincide
as the planets coincide
    the sun blinks
as the sun blinks
    the universe laughs
as the universe laughs
    I move one grain of sand

Transcendence & Art

Transcendence is the function of art: the function of drawing our attention back to the moment: the moment as transcendence. The small self is attached to time—to allow the large self is to transcend time: to experience meaning outside words.

all things are
    other
things
your-self
    included

not two

circa early 90s

*short stories
from Toadhouse*

it came down a rope
into the room
but the room was closed
and the rope was long
the sequence extended

nothing more could be thought
of
and as one might have expected
it remained over again
with time

it leads—the path
to places seem constantly
yet over and again refused
as notice—for notice
requires that we take—so
much so that most of us
are not willing to give

on the front porch
lay a feather
it lay there very still
the wind had not found it
the porch didn't mind
the feather was light
and stillness
served its purpose

the moon wandering
through the night
reflecting on light
not its own—knowing each
thing individually
positions
avoiding

squatting behind a bush
the lord of the manor
never realized that all
he left behind would
contribute to equality
with time

confused it wandered
right up to the door left
open—given to staying
the decision to leave was
more than it could take
all around was openness
a feeling it dreaded with
the beginning—that and
all

a bowl round and deep
hollow to one direction
took fright
when it realized
that all it knew
was inside

it was a fine sunny
afternoon when a squirrel
jumped on a rock   the
rock   crazed for attention
rolled to the left
leaving the squirrel
in the right

the bird taken to flight
kept the air close
around it—each wing
seemingly free at the tip
growing toward the center

the bird loved the air
although it had to take
it for granted

a relative prospect
gave rise to an opinion
the situation arose finding
comparisons necessary
the whole thing terminated
in an idea which missed
the point
entirely

the stairs led by each
to the following place

the surface contributed
to the distance—but
by and by opportunity
was past

the tea pot had seen it
all—come and go
hot cold—it didn't
matter
the spout left reason
to doubt

a leaf at the top
of a tree found life swell

birds sang to it and
the sun gave it first light

time severed the base
—and the leaf
fell with the sound

the symbol kept confusing
itself with the metaphor

the trail was well worn
so it should have been easy
but that was the problem
you see

walled in—the house took
responsibility for each
room—keeping the space
required as close as it
could—having as little
consideration as possible
not leaving any room for
the outside

if it was going to be a
book each page had to assume
itself as   separate—
relationship was necessary
but expendable with the
mean time—binding was
easily realized and in the
end a complete volume was
produced without considering
a proper attitude for eventual
meaning

deep within the earth a
hole was well placed
the idea seemed content
with a bucket

they were told that the
light they saw was dead
dead for millions of years
their eyes perceive only
the past—all that is seen
has already been—this
stopped them in their tracks

the woman was able
to be herself—she had
every reason to lack doubt
seeing her body in the mirror
reflecting as life's will

moving fluidly along up
moist pliable—the tongue
takes its relative position
in the mouth—words—forming
over and again tasting the
many levels of life's
displacement

looking for the truth among
the many things a man walked
around in circles

not looking up he never
realized the vast im-
possibilities of direction

it is a curious thing thought
closed to the eyes and with touch
not heard in its proper
sense—nor appreciated
as taste   just smell

light—thought it was being
followed (round and round)
it went examining all—
not denying a
thing at last heading
home content—beyond
the shadow of
doubt

limbo lived a life felt
by many but recognized by
few—it was a long life
by short standards—with
no belonging in sight
limbo could only hope
which contributed to its
lack of identity—this
created a sought
after description

the cup was being filled
satisfaction was close at
hand   the cup valued its
use and through it
knew the intimacy of lips
in a way we can only envy

frankly   the first time
I saw it it was un-
recognizable   that didn't
appear to bother it for
it kept its own council and
regarded the rest of us as
distinct

two hands met
creating one sound
unheard of in
retrospect

the moment rising
out of absence

there was a lively resemblance
it gave all it could
to appearances
so near was the actual that
distance couldn't take
part

like leaves

(extracts)

1993

We are
    consciousness

crotch born

a
specified form
   in
    an un-
specified
existence

it is the Body
that
    is useful

the transitory
    statement
    flush with
    existence

the subtle
draw
    of skin

lying down
with the
    horizon

setting
with the
    sun

with desire
everything
becomes a
place

on a
stem
    sweet
    smell
born to a
breeze

a flower turning
toward   its
own light……….a
reflection   held
of itself

there is nowhere
that can be completely
gone
to

nor remain
un-
attended

being—
a motion
unsurpassed

interpretation

fall
like
 leaves

asking the relationship
of all things
a fly lands on my arm

I swat at it

living
through the
motions

fashioned from darkness
with light
in mind   the affectation
of duality the fabrication
of thought

moving among
the
    many

life doubles
as
    emotion

    within the grasp
       of an eye
  form
     is taken
        back

a *leveling*
of
    consciousness
    the grey scale
of
    seeming

the number of things
we know
    are
accountable

loved and adorned
with the
    complexity
of form
idea
    finds **place**

the thought
    in passing
the pressure
    of flesh
the standard
    of time

we live
    through
appearances

there is no sense
to the beauty of
it nor the terror
of ignorance and
the disquieting
love that moves
the body beyond
comprehension

phallacy

(extracts)

1994

*facing distortion
with an open
mind*

life
takes
place

the
estate
of mind

hands reach
for direction

each day a
wandering
    past

there is a wonderful story
about a woman who believed
the world was complete and
beautiful and only she was in-
complete and ugly—she went
through life praising all that she
saw until the day she died a com-
plete and beautiful death

moon
lit
field
   alone
      red
      tipped
      Cain

curious
what words
   mean

this word
that tree
this you
that me

we go courting

*let's use an idea to
describe something
small*

rinse with
clear water
that which
is
    un-
clear

*"any thought at all
means trouble"*

the wise monk said

now
that
was
using his
head

"he covered his ears to steel the bell"
and
came to
   mind

life
is
a
prism

break in

from a notebook

2000

physical memory
(memory as experience as memory as
experienced at the time)

the ability to return as experience
(memory)
does memory again create a new
memory?
(return implies memory)

I look at a tree
the tree looks at me
reflection

art must transcend description—release bias to satisfy function

is description the excrement of thought?

is excrement what doesn't stay in the body?
dung—urine—exhalation—(ideas (thought) description)

poets and other righters

bloom to the last

we are what we don't re-cognize

life might be easier un-said

from a notebook

2002

Concepts have a function
but should never be confused with the
truth

Plastic bag over a baby's head—the air
becomes stale
And eventually the child suffocates

We are all children of the moment
Concepts risk suffocation if we
place the wrong value on them

Use them and then release them
Keep the air around the moment
<u>Fresh</u>

Concepts are like an ax to cut wood
They are not the wood

The truth is a ghost—shifts shapes
always different—shape/form is
communication. Communication must
stay open
The body obeys gravity—we are held
within form. Thought/ideas are also
form—form free from gravity—ideas are
like shooting stars—are UFOs.
Thought/ideas must move on—must
keep moving to be alive

We are born and we die the <u>between</u>
is the <u>middle mystery</u>—we are always
between
Location is the moment—there is
no way to hold on— movement is
illusion—is the moment—is the truth

<u>Illusion</u> is <u>truth</u> as <u>form</u>

<u>cozy up</u>

these words these ideas connect us
to the universe or rather explain our
connection—in fact we are inseparable
from all that is and isn't and the more
we realize this the healthier we are at all
levels—and we no longer fear death—
for death is not the end—it is but a
pause and change of characters

my body is an out of mind
experience (I think
who is this—drilling holes
pulling teeth—wanting
to know my deepest thoughts
shining light blurring
vision—passing time as
if standing still)

from a notebook

2003-2004

<u>make nothing out of sense</u>

you think I sound cosmic?
lick my lips

    ambivalence
    driver—
meaning does not exist prior
to connection
    (stars point—short comings)

does distance bother you?

no excuse for looking up

life is a perfect example of what
we were just talking about

the trouble with language
is its meaning

mouth open
    staring into space

she took off her socks
to put others on

reality is a shortcoming

a man is discussing
something with his hands

a woman with her father
2 yrs old possibly

another in her 60s
I'd say

a trite cosmic reality

culture serves time

it makes little difference
what you call it—

a technical look
that refuses forgiveness

the river flows past noon

the famous black hat
would perform in square yards

the entire local populace
would always turn out

pink is faintly reminiscent

it will take just as long
being visually critical

not knowing which way was up
I laid on my back
facing forward

it looks like a table
with words on it

two spoke softly
to each other
under the cover of flesh

economy wait—clear
protectors

under passes this way
sequencing over (time)
as new
if it knew—it would pass for ever
like new
there is a tendency to bend
around corners unless
otherwise up right

this is corroboration
unfortunately—indiscreetly

between is always
in the same space as before

(vertical makes the horizontal cross)

(speaking softly to each other)

speaking softly to each (other)
under the cover of flesh

relinquish all answers

the word
　　wood
　knows no
　　other

my thumb keeps getting
in the way

your voice becomes
as the hand
that is dealt
end of an arm

death
is bigger
than life

point penetrating
the erraticism
of distance

death
is a sure thing
bet on it!

no information
without uncertainty
and no information
worth having
without redundancy

non-simple
non-certain

A PARTIAL LIST OF SNUGGLY BOOKS

G. ALBERT AURIER *Elsewhere and Other Stories*
JULES BARBEY D'AUREVILLY *Hannibal's Ring*
S. HENRY BERTHOUD *Misanthropic Tales*
LÉON BLOY *The Tarantulas' Parlor and Other Unkind Tales*
ÉLÉMIR BOURGES *The Twilight of the Gods*
JAMES CHAMPAGNE *Harlem Smoke*
FÉLICIEN CHAMPSAUR *The Latin Orgy*
FÉLICIEN CHAMPSAUR
   The Emerald Princess and Other Decadent Fantasies
BRENDAN CONNELL *Clark*
BRENDAN CONNELL *Unofficial History of Pi Wei*
RAFAELA CONTRERAS *The Turquoise Ring and Other Stories*
ADOLFO COUVE *When I Think of My Missing Head*
QUENTIN S. CRISP *Aiaigasa*
QUENTIN S. CRISP *Graves*
LADY DILKE *The Outcast Spirit and Other Stories*
CATHERINE DOUSTEYSSIER-KHOZE *The Beauty of the Death Cap*
ÉDOUARD DUJARDIN *Hauntings*
BERIT ELLINGSEN *Now We Can See the Moon*
BERIT ELLINGSEN *Vessel and Solsvart*
ENRIQUE GÓMEZ CARRILLO *Sentimental Stories*
EDMOND AND JULES DE GONCOURT *Manette Salomon*
REMY DE GOURMONT *From a Faraway Land*
GUIDO GOZZANO *Alcina and Other Stories*
EDWARD HERON-ALLEN *The Complete Shorter Fiction*
RHYS HUGHES *Cloud Farming in Wales*
J.-K. HUYSMANS *Knapsacks*
COLIN INSOLE *Valerie and Other Stories*
JUSTIN ISIS *Pleasant Tales II*
JUSTIN ISIS (editor) *Marked to Die: A Tribute to Mark Samuels*
JUSTIN ISIS AND DANIEL CORRICK (editors)
   Drowning in Beauty: The Neo-Decadent Anthology

VICTOR JOLY *The Unknown Collaborator and Other Legendary Tales*
MARIE KRYSINSKA *The Path of Amour*
BERNARD LAZARE *The Gate of Ivory*
BERNARD LAZARE *The Mirror of Legends*
BERNARD LAZARE *The Torch-Bearers*
MAURICE LEVEL *The Shadow*
JEAN LORRAIN *Errant Vice*
JEAN LORRAIN *Fards and Poisons*
JEAN LORRAIN *Masks in the Tapestry*
JEAN LORRAIN *Monsieur de Bougrelon and Other Stories*
JEAN LORRAIN *Nightmares of an Ether-Drinker*
JEAN LORRAIN *The Soul-Drinker and Other Decadent Fantasies*
ARTHUR MACHEN *N*
ARTHUR MACHEN *Ornaments in Jade*
CAMILLE MAUCLAIR *The Frail Soul and Other Stories*
CATULLE MENDÈS *Bluebirds*
CATULLE MENDÈS *For Reading in the Bath*
CATULLE MENDÈS *Mephistophela*
ÉPHRAÏM MIKHAËL *Halyartes and Other Poems in Prose*
LUIS DE MIRANDA *Who Killed the Poet?*
OCTAVE MIRBEAU *The Death of Balzac*
TERESA WILMS MONTT *In the Stillness of Marble*
TERESA WILMS MONTT *Sentimental Doubts*
CHARLES MORICE *Babels, Balloons and Innocent Eyes*
DAMIAN MURPHY *Daughters of Apostasy*
DAMIAN MURPHY *The Star of Gnosia*
KRISTINE ONG MUSLIM *Butterfly Dream*
PHILOTHÉE O'NEDDY *The Enchanted Ring*
YARROW PAISLEY *Mendicant City*
URSULA PFLUG *Down From*
ADOLPHE RETTÉ *Misty Thule*
JEAN RICHEPIN *The Bull-Man and the Grasshopper*
DAVID RIX *A Blast of Hunters*
DAVID RIX *A Suite in Four Windows*

FREDERICK ROLFE (Baron Corvo) *Amico di Sandro*
FREDERICK ROLFE (Baron Corvo)
  An Ossuary of the North Lagoon and Other Stories
JASON ROLFE *An Archive of Human Nonsense*
BRIAN STABLEFORD (editor)
  Decadence and Symbolism: A Showcase Anthology
BRIAN STABLEFORD (editor) *The Snuggly Satyricon*
BRIAN STABLEFORD *The Insubstantial Pageant*
BRIAN STABLEFORD *Spirits of the Vasty Deep*
BRIAN STABLEFORD *The Truths of Darkness*
COUNT ERIC STENBOCK *Love, Sleep & Dreams*
COUNT ERIC STENBOCK *Myrtle, Rue & Cypress*
COUNT ERIC STENBOCK *The Shadow of Death*
COUNT ERIC STENBOCK *Studies of Death*
MONTAGUE SUMMERS *The Bride of Christ and Other Fictions*
GILBERT-AUGUSTIN THIERRY *The Blonde Tress and The Mask*
GILBERT-AUGUSTIN THIERRY *Reincarnation and Redemption*
DOUGLAS THOMPSON *The Fallen West*
TOADHOUSE *Gone Fishing with Samy Rosenstock*
TOADHOUSE *Living and Dying in a Mind Field*
RUGGERO VASARI *Raun*
JANE DE LA VAUDÈRE *The Demi-Sexes and The Androgynes*
JANE DE LA VAUDÈRE *The Double Star and Other Occult Fantasies*
JANE DE LA VAUDÈRE *The Mystery of Kama and Brahma's Courtesans*
JANE DE LA VAUDÈRE *The Priestesses of Mylitta*
JANE DE LA VAUDÈRE *Syta's Harem and Pharaoh's Lover*
JANE DE LA VAUDÈRE *Three Flowers and The King of Siam's Amazon*
JANE DE LA VAUDÈRE *The Witch of Ecbatana and The Virgin of Israel*
AUGUSTE VILLIERS DE L'ISLE-ADAM *Isis*
RENÉE VIVIEN AND HÉLÈNE DE ZUYLEN DE NYEVELT
  Faustina and Other Stories
RENÉE VIVIEN *Lilith's Legacy*
RENÉE VIVIEN *A Woman Appeared to Me*
KAREL VAN DE WOESTIJNE *The Dying Peasant*

Lightning Source UK Ltd.
Milton Keynes UK
UKHW010638280120
357742UK00001B/134